DATE DUE

Joseph STALIN

DAVID DOWNING

Heinemann Library
Chicago, Illinois

Customer Service 888-454-2279

Visit our website at www.heinemannlibrary.com

Designed by AMR
Illustrated by Art Construction
Originated by Dot Gradations
Printed in China

05 04 03 02 01
10 9 8 7 6 5 4 3 2 1

Library of Congress Cataloging-in Publication Data
Downing, David.
    Joseph Stalin / David Downing.
        p. cm. -- (Leading lives)
    ISBN 1-58810-165-7
    1. Stalin, Joseph, 1879-1953--Juvenile literature. 2. Heads of
state--Soviet Union--Biography--Juvenile literature. 3. Soviet
Union--History--1917-1936--Juvenile literature. 4. Soviet
Union--History--1936-1953--Juvenile literature. [1. Stalin, Joseph,
1879-1953. 2. Heads of state. 3. Soviet Union--History--1925-1953.] I.
Title. II. Series.

DK268.S8 D67 2001
947.084'2'092--dc21
                                                           00-012841

Acknowledgments
The publishers would like to thank the following for permission to reproduce photographs:
AKG, pp. 5, 47, 48; Corbis, pp. 6, 22, 23, 54; David King, pp. 7, 36; Hulton Getty, pp. 8, 11, 17, 19, 45; Novosti, pp. 4, 12, 15, 20, 25, 30, 31, 33, 43, 50; PA Photos, p. 55; Popperfoto, pp. 28, 34, 35, 39, 51.

Cover photograph reproduced with permission of Hulton Getty.

Our thanks to Christopher Gibb for his comments in the preparation of this book.

Every effort has been made to contact copyright holders of any material reproduced in this book. Any omissions will be rectified in subsequent printings if notice is given to the publishers.

Some words are shown in bold, **like this.** You can find out what they mean by looking in the glossary.

Contents

1 The Man of Steel

Imagine Red Square on a beautiful autumn day in Moscow in October 1935. It is the eighteenth anniversary of the Russian Revolution, and thousands upon thousands of marchers are parading through the square. Some carry portraits of Vladimir Ilyich Lenin, the leader of that revolution, but many more are holding up huge pictures of another man, one with dark, slicked-back hair, a large moustache, and narrowed eyes.

This man is standing on a platform below the high walls and soaring towers of Moscow's **Kremlin** fortress. Since 1929, he has ruled the new Russia, the Soviet Union, virtually alone. His name is Stalin, which means "man of steel" in Russian.

When he dies in 1953 he will be remembered as the maker of modern Russia, and as one of the most murderous **dictators** in history. But at this moment, in 1935, the radio and the

newspapers never stop singing his praises. They call him the "shining sun of humanity," "the father of us all," "Lenin's closest collaborator," and "the greatest man of all times, all epochs, all peoples."

▲ *A military parade in Moscow's Red Square formed part of the 1935 May Day celebrations.*

What crosses Stalin's mind when he hears such things? Does he think about his hopes for the distant future—that perfect world he claims he will one day bring about for his people? Or is he thinking about the millions who follow his orders, working long days and nights to make that future possible? Perhaps, on this day of all days, he is remembering the other men and women who shared in the making of the revolution they are celebrating, most of whom are now rotting in his jails. Or is he thinking back still further, to his own years as an outlaw, to all the nights in hiding and days on the run?

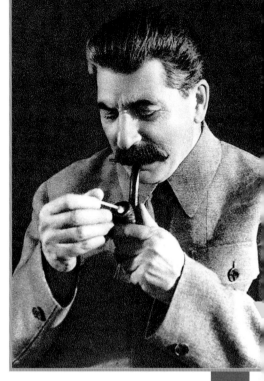

▲ Joseph Stalin, born Joseph Djugashvili, is pictured here in 1936.

Does he spare a thought for his two dead wives, his three children, or his mother far away in Soviet Georgia, who still wishes he had become a priest? Perhaps as he gazes coldly down at the marching lines of neatly uniformed schoolchildren, his mind wanders back to the long-ago days of his own childhood.

A serious case of hero worship

"All thanks to thee, O Great Educator, Stalin. I love a young woman with a renewed love and shall perpetuate myself in my children, all thanks to thee, O Great Educator, Stalin. I shall be eternally happy and joyous, all thanks to thee, O Great Educator, Stalin. Everything belongs to thee, chief of our great country. And when the woman I love presents me with a child the first word it shall utter will be 'Stalin.'"

(From a **delegate's** speech to the Soviet parliament, 1935)

2 Childhood and Youth

▲ *Stalin grew up in this small, two-room house in the Georgian town of Gori.*

On December 6, 1878, a third son was born to Vissarion and Ektarina Djugashvili in Gori, a small town in the Russian province of Georgia. Their first two boys had died as babies, but this one, called Soso (Georgian for Joseph), survived.

Vissarion earned his living making shoes at home for a business in the Georgian capital, Tiflis, but he also drank too much, and times were never easy in the small, two-room house that the family shared. It was Ektarina who made sure that the family rarely went hungry. She took in washing and did housework for wealthier families in the town. In the early years of their marriage, Vissarion frequently beat both Ektarina and Soso, but eventually Ektarina started fighting back, and Vissarion left to live in Tiflis.

Gori

The young Soso grew up in the small town, with its hot summers, rushing river, and panoramic views of snow-covered mountains. He went with his mother to the weekly market, and he watched the steam trains puff their way down the valley. At the age of 5 or 6 he caught **smallpox** and, although he survived, he was left with a permanently pock-marked face.

He started at the town's church school, where he sang in the choir, enjoyed boxing, and was considered the star pupil. He became the leader of a small gang of children, and 60 years later, at the height of World War II, he still felt fond enough of these childhood friends to send them all money. These were probably the happiest years of his life.

His father disappeared completely when Soso was about eleven, and his mother was left to make the decisions about his future. She wanted him to become a priest, partly because she was religious herself, partly because it was one of the few good jobs that poor Georgian people could hope to get. She fixed him up with a place at the most important religious school in Georgia—the Tiflis theological seminary—and his Gori headmaster helped arrange a scholarship that would pay for his clothes, food, and lodging. In 1893, at the age of 15, Soso took the train to the capital.

▶ *Soso Djugashvili (back row, fourth from the left) is pictured here with his classmates.*

The seminary

The seminary was very different from the church school. He found religious studies boring, and the discipline was much stricter than he was used to. The seminary had recently been closed for a while because of student troubles, and the teachers still did not trust their students, who were rarely allowed out into the town and were continually spied on.

Soso's rebellious instincts soon showed through. At first he was content to write fiery romantic poetry and read about the heroic adventures of Koba, a Georgian Robin Hood from years gone by, but after a year or so he became interested in more up-to-date rebels—the **Socialists.** He and other students formed a secret Socialist discussion group in the seminary, and then they joined one of the more **revolutionary** groups in the city outside. They visited groups of workers and shared their vision of a Socialist world, one that was fairer for everyone.

Soso was better at winning followers than making friends. His fellow students quickly learned that he did not like losing arguments.

▲ This is Soso Djugashvili as a student of the Tiflis seminary in 1894.

They also understood that he bore grudges against those who defeated him in discussions. He soon stopped caring about his college work, preferring to read books that were forbidden. He argued with his teachers, and was often rude. In the spring of 1899, he failed to turn up for some examinations, and the teachers used this as an excuse to expel him.

First and last job

Soso was then 20 years old, and he did not go back to Gori. That summer and autumn he did a little private teaching, and toward the end of the year he got his first and only non-political job, as a worker at the Tiflis observatory. On the night when the nineteenth century gave way to the twentieth he was alone at the telescope, taking notes on the behavior of the heavens.

Politics was the most important thing in his life. When a big demonstration was planned in the city fifteen months later, Soso was one of the main organizers. The police knew it, but when they arrived at the observatory to arrest him, he was gone. For the next sixteen years his only permanent homes would be in prison or **exile.**

"RUSSIA"

In 1900, the Russian Empire included **European Russia,** most of Poland, the vast Asian region known as Siberia, and present-day Finland, Lithuania, Latvia, Estonia, Moldova, Belarus, Ukraine, Georgia, Azerbaijan, Armenia, Turkmenistan, Kazakhstan, Uzbekistan, Kirghizstan, and Tadjikistan. Finland and Poland became independent states in 1917 and 1918. The rest remained part of the Union of Soviet Socialist Republics (or Soviet Union) until its breakup in the early 1990s.

TO LOCATE THE PLACES MENTIONED, SEE THE MAP OF THE RUSSIAN EMPIRE ON PAGE 13.

3 The Revolutionary

The first stop on Joseph Djugashvili's journey as a **revolutionary** was Batum, a small seaport on the Georgian Black Sea coast (see map on page 13). Once there he slept on the floors and sofas of sympathizers, helped print revolutionary newspapers in concealed cellars, and braved police checks with his forged documents. He gave talks to groups of workers about **Socialism,** always wondering if the police were about to come crashing through the door.

Who was Djugashvili—the future Stalin—working for? In 1898, the Russian Social Democratic Workers Party had been formed, and the small group of **Marxist Socialists,** which he had joined in Tiflis, soon became part of this bigger party. All this activity was illegal—such political parties were not allowed in the empire of the **czar.** Revolutionaries like Djugashvili thought of themselves as soldiers in a secret army, and knew that they were likely to spend much of their lives either behind bars or **exiled** to some distant Siberian outpost.

FOR DETAILS ON KEY PEOPLE OF STALIN'S TIME, SEE PAGES 58–59.

In early 1902, Djugashvili was one of the main organizers of a violent demonstration in which at least fifteen workers were killed, and the police finally caught up with him. He was locked up in Batum prison and then sent into exile. During this time, the Russian Social Democratic Workers Party split into two halves, the **Bolsheviks** and the **Mensheviks.** The Bolsheviks, under their leader Lenin, were more willing than the Mensheviks to wage a ruthless **underground war** against the authorities. When Djugashvili heard about the split he knew whose side he was on. He had no doubts that the Bolsheviks' ruthless action was what was needed.

Marxist Socialism

Karl Marx was a nineteenth-century German philosopher who believed he had worked out how society changes. He thought that throughout history each ruling class—each group of people who dominated a society through force, wealth, or a combination of the two—inevitably created its own opposition. In his time the **bourgeoisie**—the owners of industry, communications, and banks—were the ruling class in the most advanced countries, but to make their world work they needed a growing army of ordinary workers.

Marx believed that these workers would eventually get so numerous and so fed up with making wealth for other people that they would kick out the bourgeoisie and rule in their place. Since the workers would then be a big majority of the population, their rule would be fairer for most people. It would be called Socialism.

Marx had many facts to back up his theory, and many people came to believe that he was right in his predictions. They were called Marxists or Marxist Socialists.

▲ These photographs of Joseph Djugashvili—the future Stalin—were taken around 1912 or 1913 for the records of the **czarist** secret police.

First exile, first marriage

Though thin and no more than five feet and two inches (one meter and fifty-seven centimeters) tall, Djugashvili proved a brave prisoner, enduring the beatings he was given in hateful silence. After eighteen months he was exiled to the province of Irkutsk in Siberia, some 3,000 miles (4,800 kilometers) away. A first attempt at escape brought him nothing more than a frostbitten nose and ears, but the second attempt was successful, and by January 1904 he was back in Tiflis.

It was probably in this year that he met and married Ektarina Svanidze. She was the sister of another **revolutionary,** but she was religious and uninterested in politics. She insisted that they marry in church, and he agreed, even though the **Bolsheviks** were violently opposed to religion. For the next few years he seems to have led even more of a double life than he already had been. On the one hand, he tried, in almost impossible circumstances, to live a normal family life with a woman he obviously loved; on the other, he continued with his secret and always dangerous work as a revolutionary.

▲ *Stalin's first wife, Ektarina Svanidze, did not share his interest in revolutionary politics.*

Lenin's fund-raiser

The year 1905 was one of great political upheavals in the Russian Empire, but Djugashvili's part of the country was quieter than most. In December he finally met Lenin, who seems to have realized that Djugashvili was both competent and prepared to do almost anything for the party. He was given the job of raising money by carrying out robberies in his home territory of the Caucasus.

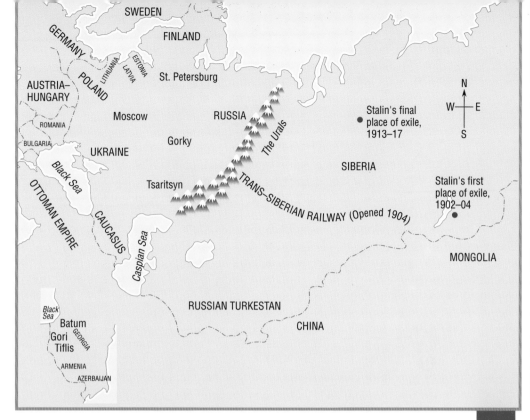

▲ This is the Russian Empire ca. 1900.

The most famous of these robberies took place in Tiflis's Erevan Square on June 26, 1907. A gold shipment and its **Cossack** guard were suddenly attacked by about 50 revolutionaries armed with bombs and guns. When the smoke cleared, many soldiers and innocent passers-by could be seen lying dead or wounded on the ground, but Djugashvili's men were gone, along with the gold.

This success, and the others that followed it, must have pleased Djugashvili, but that same year his own life was marked by tragedy. Soon after giving birth to their son Yakov, Ektarina fell ill. It was dangerous to visit her too often, and he had no money to pay for treatment. Eventually, he managed to have her moved back to her own family, but it was too late. At her funeral, Djugashvili told an old friend that she had "softened his stony heart," and that all his warm feelings for humanity had died with her.

Djugashvili left his son Yakov to be brought up by Ektarina's sister, and he threw himself back into his work. He was soon arrested. A year later he escaped, only to be recaptured after six months. Again he escaped, and again he was arrested. Each time he was sent further into the Siberian wilderness, with its long, freezing winters and short, hot summers.

Nationalities

In the winter of 1912–13, during one of his short spells of freedom, Djugashvili met Lenin in the Austrian capital, Vienna. Lenin knew that although Djugashvili was not a great speaker or thinker, he was from a poor family, and the party needed people who understood the struggle to make ends meet. Lenin particularly liked Djugashvili's no-nonsense attitude and the way he got things done. He was also useful to Lenin as a Georgian. Only two-thirds of those who lived in the Russian Empire were Russians, and if the **Bolsheviks** ever seized power they would have to deal with the other third, peoples like the Ukrainians and Armenians, Uzbeks and Georgians. Lenin asked Djugashvili to help him decide the party's policy toward these people. In early 1913, Djugashvili wrote his first important essay, "Marxism and the

Djugashvili in Vienna

"The door opened without a knock, and a strange figure appeared on the threshold: a very thin man, rather short, his face swarthy with a greyish tinge and clearly visible pockmarks. He looked anything but friendly. This stranger made a grunting sound, which might have been taken for a greeting, silently poured himself a glass of tea, and just as silently left the room."

(Leon Trotsky [see page 59] on his first sighting of his future rival, 1913)

National Question." He was now one of the party's experts and a member of its **Central Committee.** He gave himself a new name, "Stalin."

Last exile

Soon after his return to Russia, Stalin was arrested and exiled once more. World War I began in 1914, but Stalin spent most of his time fishing and hunting for the food he needed to keep himself alive. His life was often boring, usually miserable, and sometimes terrifying. One day he got lost in a blizzard and almost froze to death.

Then, early in 1917, incredible news reached Siberia—a revolution was spreading like wildfire across **European Russia.** The exiles scrambled aboard westbound trains, eager to play their part. Many of them, like Stalin, had spent their whole adult lives working and waiting for this moment.

▲ *Stalin lived in this house in Siberia during his final period in exile.*

4 Power

FOR DETAILS
ON KEY
PEOPLE OF
STALIN'S TIME,
SEE PAGES
58–59.

The revolution in February 1917 that overthrew the **czar** should, according to the predictions of Karl Marx, have been a **bourgeois** revolution, putting the business and middle classes in power. The **Socialist** revolution could only come much later, once the middle classes had developed industry and increased the number of ordinary workers. So, for the moment, it was the duty of **Marxist Socialists** to support the bourgeois revolution, and this was what Stalin and other **Bolsheviks** did once they reached the city of Petrograd **(St. Petersburg)** and began publishing the party newspaper, *Pravda* (*Truth*).

Lenin, however, had other ideas. When he reached Russia in March he wanted a complete change of policy. The Bolsheviks should aim for a Socialist revolution immediately, he announced. He agreed that Russia was not ready for one, but argued that wealthier countries like Germany were, and that a Bolshevik takeover in Russia would encourage revolution both there and everywhere else. Stalin was surprised by this change of policy, but he was tempted by the possibility of power, just as Lenin and his great ally Trotsky were.

A confusion of names

The Bolsheviks originally called themselves Marxist Socialists. According to Marx, a **Communist** society was the perfect society that would follow a Socialist one. The Bolsheviks started using the name Communists to distinguish themselves from other Socialists who were not as ready to use violence and other undemocratic methods to reach their goals. They officially changed their name to the Russian Communist Party in 1918.

If that is confusing, it may be some consolation to know that most of those involved found it confusing, too. As a result, many people mistakenly use these words interchangeably.

One Bolshevik attempt to seize power in June was defeated, but another in October proved successful. Stalin's main task in this, the second Russian revolution of 1917, was to make sure that Lenin escaped if everything went wrong. He was now a member of the party's four-man leadership committee, and someone who Lenin particularly relied on.

Civil war and new love

The Bolsheviks became the new leaders of the Russian government, but many people in Russia refused to recognize their authority. By early 1918 a **civil war** was raging between the **Red Army** (Bolsheviks) and the **White Army** (their opponents). All the normal arrangements for transporting food broke down and Stalin was sent south in an armored train to the city of Tsaritsyn. His job was to get wheat delivered to the hungry cities of Moscow and Petrograd. He had 400 **Red Guards** with him, and once in Tsaritsyn he waged a **reign of terror** against anyone involved with the **black market** in food. Thousands were shot, and many hidden grain stores were found. When a White Army attacked the city, Stalin successfully organized its defense. Seven years later it was renamed Stalingrad in his honor.

TO LOCATE THE PLACES MENTIONED, SEE THE MAP OF THE RUSSIAN EMPIRE ON PAGE 13.

▶ *This picture is of Stalin at the Eighth Congress of the Russian Communist Party in March 1919. By this time he held several important posts in both the party and the government.*

Stalin's secretary in Tsaritsyn was Nadezhda Alliluyeva, the daughter of another Bolshevik, whom Stalin had known since his Tiflis days. She was impressed by the hard and apparently romantic life he had led, and he was struck by her youth and innocence. Although there were twenty years between their ages, she became his wife.

He was sent north to Petrograd, and then south once more to the Ukraine. He seemed to have a knack for coping with military and political crises, although some of his fellow **Bolsheviks**—Trotsky in particular—thought he was unimaginative and relied too much on simple brutality. As far as Lenin was concerned, what worked was all that mattered. If the civil war was lost then they would all be slaughtered.

Positions of power

Stalin had other jobs outside of the military—jobs that became much more important once the **civil war** had been won. He was the **Commissar for Nationalities** in the government, with the responsibility of persuading the non-Russian peoples to stay within the new Soviet Union. He used both promises and threats: the non-Russians were offered partly self-governing, **autonomous** republics inside the Union, but any who tried to break away and set up their own countries quickly received a visit from the **Red Army.**

Stalin was a member of the most powerful committees in the party. He was on the ruling seven-man **Politburo** and he was a member of another committee that supervised the **political police.** Most important of all, he was a leading figure in the party Secretariat, which controlled who got what party jobs. When the post of general secretary was created early in

1922, Lenin chose Stalin to fill it, partly because no one else wanted such an apparently boring job, and partly because Lenin knew that Stalin would do it with his usual efficiency. The Georgian always got things done.

Stalin was responsible for appointing local party secretaries throughout the country. In turn, these secretaries chose the people who were sent to Moscow to serve on all the important committees. In the future, when there were disputes over policy, or disagreements about who should lead the party, Stalin would be able to count on a great deal of support.

▼ *General Secretary Stalin walks down a Moscow street with Commissar for the Economy (and fellow Georgian) Sergo Ordzhonikidze in 1924.*

5 The Succession Struggle

▲ *Stalin visited the convalescing Lenin in the village of Gorky during 1922.*

Lenin became seriously ill late in 1921, and by the middle of the following year he was forced to take a long holiday from work and responsibility. He went to stay in Gorky, a village about 20 miles (30 kilometers) south of the new capital Moscow. Stalin was his most frequent visitor.

Things were going well for the Georgian. The war was over, and he had one of the most important jobs in the country. He and Nadezhda had moved into a house in Moscow. It was the first proper home of his adult life. They had a new son, Vasili, and in 1921 Yakov, Stalin's son from his first marriage whom he had hardly seen for fifteen years, came to live with them.

Lenin's illness, however, was a dark cloud on his horizon. Stalin had always been Lenin's man, and he knew he would have to fight for his political life against the other **Bolshevik** leaders when Lenin died. He may also have discovered that Lenin now regretted giving him so much power, an issue Lenin raised in his *Testament* (a letter to the Party Congress).

Last words

*"Having become general secretary, Comrade Stalin has concentrated unlimited power in his hands, and I am not sure that he will always use that power with sufficient care. . . . Stalin is too rude and this failing, which is entirely acceptable in relations among us **Communists,** is not acceptable in a general secretary. I therefore suggest that the comrades find a means of moving Stalin from this post and giving the job to someone else who is superior to Comrade Stalin in every way, that is, more patient, more loyal, more respectful, and more considerate to his comrades. . . ."*

(Excerpts from Lenin's *Testament*, written in December 1922 and January 1923)

A narrow escape

Lenin died in January 1924, and his *Testament* was finally read to the **Central Committee** at the party's Thirteenth Congress in May. Stalin was not the only one whom Lenin criticized, but he was the only one the old leader suggested should be sacked. Most of those present were embarrassed for Stalin. "He looked small and miserable," one eyewitness wrote later, "in spite of his self-control and show of calm it was clearly evident that his fate was at stake."

This was one of the key moments of the twentieth century. Had the other leaders insisted on upholding Lenin's wishes, the future of the Soviet Union and the rest of the world would probably have been very different. But for reasons of their own they allowed him to keep his job, little realizing that one day he would use it to have them all killed.

Differences

Why did they allow Stalin to keep his power? One reason was that the other Bolshevik leaders were split along lines of both personality and policy. They did not like each other very much, and they did not agree with each other when it came to deciding what they should do next with their revolution. Trotsky was the most famous and the most able of them, but he was also the most conceited (as Lenin had pointed out in his *Testament*). The others did not like the way he talked down to them, and they were afraid he would try to use his influence with the **Red Army** to seize power on his own. Even those who agreed with Trotsky's ideas for the revolution, like the popular Zinoviev, were scared of supporting him too wholeheartedly. These people allowed Stalin to survive—at least in part—because they felt they needed him and his supporters as a counterbalance to Trotsky.

FOR DETAILS ON KEY PEOPLE OF STALIN'S TIME, SEE PAGES 58–59.

▲ *Leon Trotsky was Stalin's principal adversary in the period surrounding Lenin's death.*

There were also those, like Bukharin, who opposed Trotsky because they disagreed with his ideas. The **Bolsheviks** had originally justified their revolution by saying that it would encourage revolutions elsewhere, but these had not happened. Trotsky said that they should carry on trying to make trouble in the rest of the world (he called this a policy of "permanent

22

revolution"), but Bukharin and his allies thought the Bolsheviks should get used to the idea that they had to concentrate on their own revolution. Their job was to do whatever they could in Russia, to build "**Socialism** in one country."

Stalin supported Bukharin's policy, partly because this had also been Lenin's position, and partly because it seemed to make more practical sense than Trotsky's. In return, Bukharin and his allies were happy to offer Stalin support when he most needed it.

The way forward

Once Stalin had survived Lenin's *Testament,* he went from strong to stronger. With Bukharin and his allies he always had a majority on the important committees, and Trotsky and Zinoviev were continually outvoted. "Socialism in one country" became the party's official goal.

▲ *Stalin was accompanied here by fellow party leaders Alexei Rykov, Lev Kamenev, and Grigori Zinoviev in June 1925.*

23

Now that the goal of establishing Socialism in Russia had been decided, the leaders began arguing about how best to achieve it. The Soviet Union needed industry and workers, but the only people who could pay for the necessary expansion of Russian industry—supply the food for the cities and the labor for the factories—were the people who now lived in the countryside, the **peasants,** who still made up more than 90 percent of the population. Lenin had wanted to encourage the peasants to produce more food and make more money. He hoped that they would spend this money on **industrial goods** and thereby stimulate the expansion of industry. It would be a slow process, but he was convinced that eventually it would work.

Fast or slow?

Stalin and Bukharin continued to support this policy after Lenin's death, but Trotsky and Zinoviev thought that things should be sped up. They were not convinced that the peasants would do what was expected of them, and they were also afraid that the party, by encouraging what Trotsky called "the devil of the market," would allow the **bourgeoisie** to recover some of its power. They argued that the peasants should be paid less for their food than the **market rate.** The towns would make a profit, which they could use to build industries, and the peasants would have no choice but to come and work in them if they wanted a decent living.

This argument could be heard at hundreds of party meetings in the mid–1920s, but the "slow" approach favored by Stalin and Bukharin remained the official policy, at least for the moment. Stalin was always careful to make sure he had majority support when a vote was called for, and he was quite prepared to postpone meetings when it looked like he might lose.

He was good at arguing his case as well. He was not dramatic or clever like Trotsky, but was thorough, logical, and straightforward. He was also good at picking out quotations from Lenin's writings to support his own views.

Stalin's home life during this period also seemed secure, and in 1926 Nadezhda gave birth to a daughter, Svetlana.

One left standing

As the years went by, Stalin got more and more of his own supporters onto the **Central Committee** and the smaller **Politburo.** In early 1927, both Trotsky and Zinoviev were forced out of the leadership, and there seemed no one left to oppose the "slow" approach, no one left to threaten Stalin and Bukharin's position.

This was not enough for Stalin. With what now seems almost incredible nerve, he suddenly changed his mind and came out in favor of the very policies for which he had condemned Trotsky and Zinoviev. Now it was Bukharin and his supporters who found themselves outvoted on committees packed with Stalin's supporters. Over the next two years they were forced out of their positions, leaving only Stalin at the summit of power.

▶ *Nikolai Bukharin was Stalin's chief ally during the years 1924–29.*

Why did Stalin adopt those policies which he had so recently opposed? He certainly wanted to get rid of Bukharin, who was the only other important leader left from Lenin's day, but there were other good reasons for the change of course. The outside threats to the Soviet Union seemed to be growing, and in the modern world a country needed industrial strength to defend itself. The slow way was too slow, and in any case the peasants were refusing to cooperate with the existing system, hoarding their grain and refusing to sell it to the cities. Stalin decided that if he was going to industrialize Russia he needed to take complete control—of the countryside, of the cities, of everything and everyone.

Key dates: Stalin's rise to power

1917	The Bolshevik Revolution
1918–21	Civil war
1922	Stalin becomes general secretary
1924	Lenin dies
1925–27	Stalin defeats Trotsky and Zinoviev
1927–29	Stalin defeats Bukharin

6 Modernization

The enormous upheaval that took place in Russia between 1927 and 1932 changed the country beyond recognition. It was not called a revolution, but it was one in all the ways that mattered, and Stalin was its leader.

In these years Stalin undertook the **modernization** of Russia, but it was not this alone—the growth of industries and communications and the mechanization of agriculture—that added up to a revolution. England, Germany, the United States, and others had all been through such developments in the past. What turned Stalin's modernization program into a revolution was the way it was done. Never before had a country modernized itself at such incredible speed or with such terrible disregard for the human consequences.

Farming

The first step was to control the **peasants,** and at the end of 1927 the **collectivization of agriculture** was announced. There would be no more private farms. Peasants would become workers on one of the new, huge collective farms and would be paid a wage like any worker in the town. All animals and tools would belong to the collective. Machine tractor stations would be set up to provide tractors for each group of 40 farms. The harvest, in whole or part, would belong to the state. The local party officials would make all the decisions about what to grow and who did what jobs.

The wealthier farmers (called **kulaks**) had the most to lose, and Stalin knew that they would fight his plans. In 1929, he announced that he was going to "liquidate the kulaks as a social class," and over the next few years he kept his word.

The liquidation of the kulaks

"Trainloads of deported peasants left for the icy north, the forests, the steppes, the desert. These were whole populations, denuded of everything; the old folk starved in mid-journey, new-born babies were buried on the banks of the roadside, and each wilderness had its crop of little crosses of boughs or white wood."

(A description from *Memoirs of a Revolutionary*, written by the **revolutionary** Victor Serge)

▲ *A group of farm workers was photographed here at a collective farm near Kharkov in the Ukraine.*

Most of the **kulaks** were killed or sent to labor camps; even the luckiest ones were sent to poor farming areas. At least half a million peasants died in this first phase of **collectivization,** but many more than that died in the famines that followed. Rather than give up their animals to the collective farms, millions of peasants just killed and ate them. Rather than give up their crops, they burned them. And then they often starved.

Stalin now had the complete control over agriculture that he thought he needed to pay for industrialization. But he had made a lasting enemy of the countryside and its people, and Soviet agriculture would never really recover from these few terrible years.

Industry

The growth of industry was also completely controlled by the party. There was no room for private enterprise or market forces, and no place for individual profits or the uncertainty of uncontrolled contacts with the world economy. The Russian economy was sealed off from the rest of the world, and almost everything that happened in it—buying, selling, producing, transporting—was planned down to the last detail.

If a new steelworks was planned, then one organization was ordered to supply the bricks and machinery, another to build the necessary roads and railways, and another to ensure that enough workers were found to run the works once it was built. The central planners decided the level of wages, the sources of raw materials, and the destination of the final product. This, and every other industry, was included in one great national plan.

There had been some rough planning in Russia since 1921— some rough notion of what the country needed and how the party should go about providing it—but this sort of detailed planning, covering the whole economy over a period of years, was completely new. It had never been tried in any country.

The first **five-year plan,** which was introduced in 1928, was incredibly ambitious. Stalin tackled the basics first: he ordered a three-fold increase in the Soviet production of coal, iron, steel, oil, and machinery in those five years. Once the country had achieved this, other industries, like the weapons industry, could be expanded in their turn. Stalin had not forgotten that the rest of the world was hostile to the lone **Communist** state. "We are 50 to 100 years behind the advanced countries," he said in 1931. "We must make up this gap in ten years. Either we do this or they crush us."

◀ *These workers are using picks and shovels to modernize the village of Magnitogorsk. In 1929, it had a population of just over 1,000. Four years later it had steel mills, blast furnaces, shops, hospitals, schools, and a population of over 100,000.*

A different world

Many Soviet people wanted to see their country modernized, and there was much enthusiasm and idealism among the hundreds of thousands who set off to build new dams on the huge rivers or construct cities like Magnitogorsk from scratch in the rugged Siberian wilderness. The work was hard, and the wages poor, but the sense of achievement in transforming a country undoubtedly infected many of those involved.

Those who lacked enthusiasm still had to work. On many projects, two absences from work meant time in jail; more than that meant a spell in a **labor camp.** With everything planned to the last detail, economic freedom became a thing of the past. You worked where and how you were told. Internal passports and labor books detailing an individual's work history were introduced to stop people from moving around from place to place or job to job. Stalin's control over the life of the whole country became virtually complete.

▼ *Stalin's second wife, Nadezhda Alliluyeva, was photographed here sitting in the garden of Stalin's **dacha** around 1930.*

However, there was one person Stalin could not control. His wife Nadezhda, shocked by the sufferings in the countryside, had become deeply depressed. One evening in 1932, after an argument with Stalin in front of guests, she stormed off to her room and shot herself. Stalin showed no grief for her death. Perhaps he had learned by this time to hide his feelings. Perhaps he no longer had any to hide.

7 Terror

Many people had their lives turned inside out by the **collectivization of agriculture** and the forced industrialization program that began at the end of the 1920s. Some lost their land and their independence, and nearly everyone lost the freedom to do what they wanted and go where they wanted. Those who protested were arrested, and more often than not they ended up in prison or a **labor camp.** In 1930, a special department of the secret police was set up to run the growing number of camps. This department was called the Gulag.

Conditions in the labor camps were terrible. Most of the camps were situated in Siberia or the far north of **European Russia,** where the winters were long, dark, and incredibly cold. The prisoners were forced to work long hours for pitifully small rations, and many died of hunger, **hypothermia,** or simple exhaustion. In the early 1930s, most of those sent to the camps were ordinary criminals, **peasants** who had opposed the collectivization, or workers who had failed to do the work required of them. But from 1934 onward, these groups were quickly outnumbered by the victims of the **purges.**

Kirov

Stalin had now been the country's undisputed leader for several years, and he must have felt more alone than ever. His wife was dead and he had fallen out with his older son Yakov, whom he considered weak. He hardly saw Vasili and Svetlana, his two children by Nadezhda. In the 1920s, he had often spent evenings with his comrades and their wives, but after Nadezhda's death the wives were no longer invited. He now spent his time alone or with people who dared not contradict him. Everyone said they were loyal to him, but what were they saying behind his back? He worried that he had no real way of finding out what was going on.

▲ *Stalin was photographed here with his two children by his second wife, Nadezhda: Vasili (born in 1921) and Svetlana (born in 1926). By the mid–1930s, Stalin hardly spent any time with his children.*

Then, at the Seventeenth Congress of the Russian Communist Party in early 1934, a surprising number of party members voted against his policies. Many were worried that the industrialization and collectivization programs were going too fast, and that the cost in human lives was too high. There was even talk of replacing Stalin with Sergei Kirov, the popular leader of the party's Leningrad **(St. Petersburg)** branch.

Stalin felt threatened, both personally and politically. Since he felt certain that his policies were the right ones, he could convince himself that any attack on him was also an attack on the country's future. It seems likely that he was actually fond of Kirov, but he was not going to let human feelings get in the way of protecting his own, and the Soviet Union's, interests.

◀ Stalin was photographed here with Leningrad party boss Sergei Kirov. Stalin used Kirov's assassination as his excuse for launching the Great Terror.

On December 1, 1934, Kirov was shot dead in Leningrad. No indisputable evidence has ever been found to connect Stalin with the murder, but most people believe that he was behind it. In one stroke he had gotten rid of his biggest rival and created the excuse for going after all the others who had dared to oppose him at the Seventeenth Congress.

Years of fear

FOR DETAILS ON KEY PEOPLE OF STALIN'S TIME, SEE PAGES 58–59.

Over the next five years, in what came to be called the Great **Purge** or Great Terror, millions of party members and officials were either sent to the camps or executed. Old colleagues of Stalin like Zinoviev and Bukharin, who had already been removed from positions of power, were now given public **"show trials"** in which they confessed to all sorts of ridiculous crimes that they had not actually committed. There were several explanations for these confessions. Some confessed to save their families, some because they hoped to save themselves, and some because they still wanted to believe that the party they had supported all their lives could not be wrong. They were all found "guilty" and executed.

These show trials were just the tip of the iceberg. Fear gripped the whole country, and many people took this opportunity to settle old scores. Neighbors reported neighbors, and children reported their own parents. It was no longer safe to say what you thought to anyone. Thousands of people heard the dreaded knock on their doors in the middle of the night that meant the secret police had come to take them away. Even Trotsky, now far away in Mexico, was tracked down and killed. If Stalin was to sleep safely in his bed, then no one else could.

▲ Workers at a Moscow factory listened as an official read a party bulletin denouncing Bukharin and his codefendants at the 1938 show trial.

▲ *This Russian magazine cover showed Stalin as a star in the sky.*

A man alone

With the **reign of terror** came the **personality cult.** Stalin was everything and everywhere. His face appeared on billboards and covered whole buildings. It was even projected onto the clouds above. His bust or portrait adorned offices, factories, and ordinary living rooms. Factories, streets, hospitals, rivers, and towns were named after him. Plays, films, poems, and novels celebrated his "universal genius." He was there to look after his children (the people of Russia) in whatever way they deserved. God-like, he offered a clear choice: the heaven of working for a **Communist** future or the hell of the **labor camps.**

Who was the man inside this self-proclaimed god? The one thing we know is that he was essentially alone, and remained that way until the end. He traveled in his bulletproof limousine along roads that had been cleared of people, and arrived by train at empty, echoing station platforms. He had more than ten homes, each with its staff of servants forever waiting for an unannounced arrival.

Stalin's trip to the cinema

"One day Stalin decides to go to the cinema in disguise and hear what people are really saying about him. When the newsreel comes on the audience stands up and applauds each time he appears on the screen. Stalin is pleased. Modestly, he himself stays seated. After a few moments the man next to him leans over and whispers: 'Most people feel the same way you do, Comrade, but you'll be safer if you stand up.'"

(A Russian joke from the 1930s)

Stalin spent most of his days working and brooding at either the **Kremlin** or one of his country houses, or **dachas.** Most of his evenings featured long social dinners with the men he trusted most—party leaders like Molotov, Voroshilov, Kaganovich, and Beria, who owed their positions completely to him. He liked watching movies, and was particularly fond of Charlie Chaplin, but he had few other hobbies or interests. He could have had anything he wanted in the way of luxuries, but such things did not interest him. He was only really interested in power over others, and the contentment he derived from that was always tinged with the fear that it might be taken away.

Inhuman

"He is unhappy at not being able to convince everyone, himself included, that he is greater than everyone else, and this unhappiness of his may be his most human trait, perhaps the only human trait in him. But what is not human . . . is that because of this unhappiness he cannot avoid taking revenge on people . . . if someone speaks better than he does, that man is for it! Stalin will not let him live, because that man is a constant reminder that he, Stalin, is not the first and the best. . . ."

(The words of Nikolai Bukharin, 1936)

8 War

By the end of the 1930s, Stalin's position inside his own country was stronger than it had ever been, but the spread of his **purges** to the **Red Army** from 1937 to 1939—which involved the shooting of thousands of officers—seriously weakened the country's ability to defend itself. This was particularly dangerous at a time when the threats from outside—particularly from the strong and violently anti-**Communist** Nazi Germany—seemed to be growing almost daily.

Playing for time

Stalin did his best to counter these threats. After 1934, he encouraged **Communists** in foreign countries to join with others on the left in **anti-Fascist popular fronts.** In 1936, he sent "volunteers" to fight against the **Fascists** in the **Spanish Civil War.** He tried to create an anti-German alliance with the British and French. But all these efforts failed, and the Germans grew ever stronger and more dangerous.

When the British and French did not even invite the Soviet Union to the **Munich Conference** in 1938, Stalin became convinced that they were trying to push the Germans eastward, against his own country. He responded a year later by signing the **Nazi–Soviet Pact** with Germany, which he expected would have the opposite effect, and entangle Germany in a war with Britain and France. This, he calculated, would give him more time to repair the damage done to the Red Army by the purges. The division of Poland between Germany and the Soviet Union, which had been included in the Pact, also meant moving the Russian border 200 miles (320 kilometers) to the west. If the Germans did attack Russia in the future, their troops would have further to go to reach Moscow.

▲ *German Foreign Minister von Ribbentrop, Joseph Stalin, and Soviet Foreign Minister Molotov met at the signing of the Nazi–Soviet Pact in August 1939.*

Shock and recovery

There is no reason to think that Stalin expected the Pact to last forever, but he probably hoped that the British and French would keep the Germans occupied for longer than two years. He was certainly far from ready when the Germans did attack the Soviet Union in June 1941, and seems to have spent several days trying to persuade himself that it was not really happening. He had ignored warnings from the British in the days leading up to the attack, and he failed to give any clear instructions to his commanders at the front line. When the Germans easily broke through the Soviet lines and took hundreds of thousands of prisoners, he fell into a rage, blaming everyone but himself. He had many generals shot.

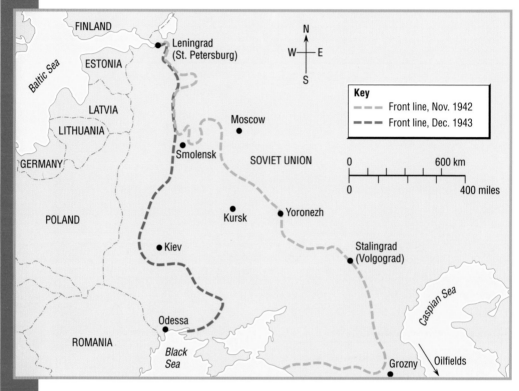

▲ *This map illustrates Germany's attack on the Soviet Union.*

It was almost two weeks before he spoke to the Soviet people, but when he did he succeeded in striking the right note. "Comrades, citizens, brothers, and sisters," he began, as if the Russian people were one big family. He did not tell his listeners they were fighting for **Communism,** or **collectivization of agriculture,** or his own "universal genius"—he told them they were fighting a "Great Patriotic War" for eternal Mother Russia, just like the one their ancestors had fought against Napoleon and the French 130 years earlier. Napoleon had failed and so would Hitler. The Russian people would never surrender.

During these first terrible months of the war, when the German armies looked unstoppable, one of the many Soviet officers captured was Stalin's son Yakov. The Germans offered to exchange him for some of their captured officers, but Stalin refused. In his eyes, Yakov had failed, becoming a traitor by letting himself be captured, and Stalin disowned him. Yakov killed himself in captivity not long afterward.

Running the war

As summer gave way to autumn, an early German victory looked more and more likely. Three things prevented it. One was the arrival of the earliest winter in living memory, which first clogged the roads with mud and then with snow, slowing the tanks to a crawl. A second was the Germans' own behavior. In many areas they were welcomed, but they treated everyone so viciously that soon even Stalin's **dictatorship** looked good by comparison.

Stalin was lucky on both these counts, but he could claim some credit for the third block to the Germans' progress—the **Red Army's** ability to fight on, despite losing so much territory and so many industrial plants. It was able to do so because most of the armament factories had been moved east of Moscow, where they were still a long way beyond the Germans' reach.

In late November, the Germans were thrown back from the outer suburbs of Moscow. It is hard to say whether Stalin's decision to stay in the **Kremlin** through these critical days inspired the Red Army units defending the capital, but it does seem fairly certain that his departure would have dealt a terrible blow to their confidence.

Stalin was far from a physical coward, and he also proved himself quite competent when it came to military strategy. Early in the campaign a state defense committee, *Stavka*, was set up to run the Soviet war machine, with Stalin, needless to say, at its head. This committee made all the key military decisions over the next three and a half years, and since most of these proved reasonably good decisions, Stalin deserves some credit as a war leader. If he did not always know what to do himself, he was good at picking and listening to generals who did.

Stalingrad and after

When the Germans launched a huge attack in the spring of 1942, the Soviets did not repeat their mistake of 1941. Instead of trying to hold its ground and ending up encircled by German tanks, the **Red Army** simply retreated, drawing the enemy further and further into the vast open spaces of the Soviet Union. Hitler was determined that his armies should take the city of Stalingrad, thinking that this would be a symbolic defeat for Stalin himself.

The Red Army lured the Germans on, until there were almost half a million men fighting each other in the ruins of the city. And then the trap was sprung. In November, more Soviet armies, supplied with tanks and guns from the factories that had been moved to the east, encircled and cut off the German troops. Two horrifying months later they surrendered. It was a blow from which the German army never really recovered.

From that moment on, the Red Army's eventual triumph was never really in doubt. There were a few temporary setbacks, but the Germans were steadily forced back toward their own

▲ These soldiers of the Red Army were fighting amidst the ruins of Stalingrad in October 1942. Three months later the surrender of the German army trapped in the city signaled a turning point of the war.

borders and beyond. In April 1945, the Red Army finally captured the German capital, Berlin. By this time Stalin had long since left the day-to-day direction of the armies to his generals. He was concentrating on making sure that the Soviets did well in the coming peace.

Key dates: World War II in Russia

1941	• June–Nov.	The Germans advance 600 miles (960 kilometers) into Soviet territory, but are stopped outside Moscow and Leningrad. The siege of Leningrad will last 900 days.
1942	• June–Nov.	German advance in the south fails to reach the Caucasus oil fields or capture Stalingrad
	• Nov.–Jan. 1943	A large German army is cut off and captured in Stalingrad. From this point on the Red Army holds the initiative.
1943	• July–Aug.	The battle of Kursk, the greatest tank battle in history, is won by the Red Army
1943	• Dec.– April 1945	The Red Army throws the Germans out of the Soviet Union and drives them all the way to Berlin

During the war, vast areas of **European Russia** and the Ukraine had been laid to waste, and farms, industries, and communications were completely destroyed. After the dramatic progress of the 1930s, it seemed as if the country was almost back to square one. The Soviet Union needed a huge rebuilding program, and that could only be carried through if the country was not being threatened from outside. Stalin's first objective at the peace negotiations was therefore to make his country safe. The most important things he wanted were a weak, divided Germany and friendly governments in the European countries, like Poland and Romania, that bordered his own.

Wishful thinking and misunderstandings

In Britain and the U.S. there was much good will toward Stalin and the Soviet people. Most people in the West realized how much the Soviet Union had suffered at the Germans' hands, and Stalin himself—or "Uncle Joe" as he was often affectionately known—was considered a heroic figure. Few people in the West knew the extent of Stalin's crimes inside the Soviet Union, and there was a great reluctance to think of him as a new enemy, or to worry about the possibility of another war, this time between themselves and the Soviet Union.

Three conferences were held by the Big Three powers (Britain, the U.S., and the Soviet Union) to decide the shape of the postwar world—at Tehran in Iran in 1943, at Yalta in the Crimea (now Ukraine) in 1945, and at Potsdam in Germany in 1945. At each of these meetings Stalin and the Western leaders reached informal agreements that seemed to satisfy them. But in the end these agreements proved worthless for one simple reason—they were based on the idea that all the powers could get what they needed and wanted. They couldn't. It was like telling two people they could each have a room, when there was only one room to begin with. You could have a Poland that was friendly to the Soviet Union or you could have a Poland that was part of a **free enterprise** Europe. You could not have both.

For several months after the war the two sides tried to convince themselves and each other that everything would work out. At the Yalta conference, Stalin had promised that he would not support **Communists** in countries like Greece, which lay outside those areas he considered crucial for the security of the Soviet Union, and he kept those promises. All over the world the war had given a boost to local Communist parties, and the situation was much more promising for world revolution than it had been in the early 1920s. But Stalin remained faithful to "**Socialism** in one country," and did virtually nothing to help them.

▼ *Stalin represented the Soviet Union and Winston Churchill represented Britain at Yalta in 1945.*

Dividing up the world

"I wrote out on a half-sheet of paper:
Romania: Russia 90%, others 10%
Greece: Great Britain (in accord with U.S.) 90%, Russia 10%
Yugoslavia: 50–50%
Hungary: 50–50%
Bulgaria: Russia 75%, the others 25%.
I pushed this across to Stalin . . . there was a slight pause.
Then he took his blue pencil and made a large tick upon it
and passed it back to us. It was all settled in no more time
than it takes to set it down."

(Winston Churchill, remembering the way he and Stalin
divided up eastern Europe at a Moscow meeting in October 1944)

Accepting the inevitable

It slowly became clear to Stalin that the North Americans
were not playing ball. They had agreed to share the secret of
how to make the atomic bomb but now refused to do so,
even though many important people in both Britain and the
U.S. thought that they should. In the summer of 1945, they
suddenly stopped sending **Lend-Lease** aid to the Soviet
Union. When, two years later, they offered more economic
help as part of their **Marshall Plan** package for the whole of
Europe, they asked Stalin to accept conditions that he found
both insulting and threatening. These included opening Russia
to Western inspectors and a guarantee of American property
rights in eastern Europe. And when the Americans tried to
bribe the Poles and Romanians into accepting similar
conditions it looked as if they were deliberately trying to turn
the Soviet Union's neighbors into the Soviet Union's enemies.
Stalin fought back. The **Red Army** was still occupying most

▲ An American transport plane was photographed coming in to land at Berlin's Tempelhof Airport in August 1948. Stalin attempted to control all of Berlin by closing the roads and railways, but he could not stop Western planes from airlifting in supplies.

of eastern Europe, and he used its presence to install **Communist** governments in one country after another. With party **dictatorships, planned economies,** and the **collectivization of agriculture,** these countries were sealed off from the free enterprise world as completely as the Soviet Union. It was the only certain way to keep them friendly.

The Americans saw this as Communist aggression, and the two sides gave up any pretense that their practical differences could be sorted out around a conference table. Instead they both began to emphasize their **ideological differences** and to compete with each other all over the world, wherever their supporters came into conflict. Stalin was probably happier with this **Cold War** than he had been with such an uncertain peace. It was his world against theirs. He could control his world, and keep theirs at a distance.

10 Final Years

The eight years that passed between the end of World War II and Stalin's death in March 1953 were years of intense economic activity in the Soviet Union. The factories, dams, and railways destroyed by the Germans were rebuilt, and new ones grew up beside them. For the second time in twenty years the Soviet people set out to lay the foundations of a prosperous future. In the Soviet media the achievements of people and party in both war and peace were continually praised and celebrated.

These really were extraordinary achievements, but Stalin took no risks. He made sure his people had nothing to compare them with. **Red Army** soldiers returning from duty in eastern Europe were forbidden to talk about what they had seen, the newspapers either ignored or lied about life in the West, and hardly any Soviet citizens were allowed to travel abroad.

МЫ ИДЕМ ДАЛЬШЕ, ВПЕРЕД, К КОММУНИЗМУ.

И. В. СТАЛИН.

The mixture as before

Stalin himself was more of a **dictator** than ever. He hardly ever appeared in public, and made few speeches. He lived mostly at one of his **dachas** outside Moscow, and took a long vacation on the Black Sea coast each autumn.

◀ *Lenin looks approvingly over Stalin's shoulder in this 1950 Soviet propaganda poster.*

There was no longer any pretense of collective (group) leadership—the ruling **Politburo** and the party's **Central Committee** did not even meet between 1947 and 1952. Stalin decided what he wanted to happen, and the necessary instructions were passed on to the Soviet people by his small band of faithful colleagues.

Stalin's touch

"When I felt his handshake it was like being struck by lightning. I hid my hand inside my coat cuff, got into my car and rushed home. Without stopping to answer my worried wife's questions I went to the cot where my small son was sleeping, stretched out my hand and rubbed his head with it, so that he too would feel the warmth of Stalin's touch."

(Yuri Borisov, an important industrial manager in the 1940s, on meeting Stalin)

At the same time his **personality cult** reached new heights of absurdity. The newspaper *Pravda* had this advice for its readers in February 1950: "If you meet with difficulties in your work, or suddenly doubt your abilities, think of him—of Stalin—and you will find the confidence you need. If you feel tired in an hour when you should not, think of him—of Stalin—and your work will go well."

But no amount of power, no extremes of praise, could make him feel safe. "Everywhere and in everything he saw 'enemies,' 'two-facers,' and 'spies,'" one of his supporters said years later. In 1948, Stalin ordered a new **purge,** and 1,000 party members were shot in Leningrad. For most of the next five years those nearest to him lived in fear. They knew only too well what had happened to Stalin's colleagues in the past.

No second chances

"The terrible thing about Stalin was that if you made a mistake with him, it was like mishandling a detonator—it was the last mistake of your life. Stalin was terrible because he never listened to excuses. He never even accused you; the only sign was a malignant gleam from his yellow, tigerish eyes and a slight puckering of his lower eyelids. Inwardly he had already passed sentence without the victim being aware of it: he would be allowed to leave, he would be arrested the same night, and by morning he would be shot."

(Russian writer Alexander Solzhenitsyn, who spent many years in Stalin's prison camps. Several of his books paint a vivid and harrowing picture of life inside these camps.)

▲ *Here, Stalin attends the Nineteenth Congress of the Russian Communist Party in October 1952.*

A bad end

Early in 1953, a group of **Kremlin** doctors was suddenly arrested and charged with the poisoning of a minor party leader some years before, and it seemed almost certain that a new and terrible **purge** was about to begin. But before this could happen, Stalin suffered the first of two strokes. Three days later, on March 5, he died.

"The death agony was terrible," his daughter said later. "He literally choked to death as we watched. At what seemed like the very last moment he suddenly opened his eyes and cast a glance over everyone in the room. It was a terrible glance, insane or perhaps angry and full of fear of death."

His colleagues hardly bothered to conceal their relief. In the country's **labor camps** the news of his death raised hopes that the long nightmare was over. For all the people of the Soviet Union it felt as if an era had ended, but after more than twenty years of Stalin-worship it was also hard to imagine the world without him. Hundreds of thousands came from all over the Soviet Union to attend his funeral, and many were killed in the mad crush of weeping mourners.

▲ A bank of flowers lined the Kremlin wall on either side of the mausoleum where Stalin's body was placed beside Lenin's in March 1953.

11 Legacy

No one knows exactly how many Soviet citizens died premature deaths while Stalin ruled. The best estimate is that between 15 and 20 million people perished during the period of **collectivization,** forced industrialization, and the great **purge** (1929–38). Some died of starvation, some from ill-treatment, and some were executed, but they all died as a direct and predictable result of Stalin's policies. He was one of the greatest mass murderers in human history.

Comparisons are often made between Stalin and the German leader Hitler, who was also criminally responsible for millions of deaths. The one obvious difference lay in their aims. Hitler looked no further than a world of masters and slaves; Stalin, at least in the beginning, believed in creating a fairer world for everyone. This does not excuse Stalin's terrible crimes, but it does make it important to understand them.

In the beginning the various ideas of Marxism, **Socialism,** and **Communism** were all concerned with bringing an end to poverty and injustice, by introducing greater equality among people, and by promoting a version of freedom that was rooted in fairness. The fact that **Marxist Socialists** took over the government of Russia meant that Socialism came to be associated with what happened in that country. So one consequence of Stalin's crimes was to discredit, or at least to raise serious doubts about, Socialism as a way forward for humanity.

Stalin's contribution

It is important to separate out Stalin's personal contribution and work out which things he alone was responsible for. Both Lenin and Trotsky were willing to use terror against their enemies, and Trotsky argued for a forced industrialization program before Stalin did. Any of the three might have introduced the system of economic planning, and allowed the death of democracy that accompanied it.

What set Stalin apart was his lack of restraint. He was not held back—as Lenin and Trotsky both were—by sympathy for other human beings, and he was always terrified of losing the power he had. These warped aspects of his personality were what cost so many millions their lives.

There was at least something in the Soviet Union to show for all the sacrifice. Fifty years of industrialization were crammed into ten, and this growth was essential to the country's success in World War II—a success that the rest of the world had good reason to be grateful for. There were also important elements of Socialism's original promise in the free universal health care and education systems that were set up, and in the guarantee of jobs for everyone.

FOR DETAILS ON KEY PEOPLE OF STALIN'S TIME, SEE PAGES 58–59.

After his death

When Stalin died his successors thought they could abandon the bad parts of his system—the **dictatorship** and the terror—and build on the achievements. At the Twentieth Party Congress in 1956, the Soviet leader Nikita Khrushchev criticized Stalin's "excesses" and announced that the party would be "de-Stalinized." But the system of central planning was not changed, and over the next twenty years it became obvious that it was not working as they had hoped. Stalin's system was good at getting modernization started, at doing simple things such as increasing steel production and building railways, but when it came to the complex economy of the late twentieth century, with its millions of different types of goods, it could not cope. There were just too many possibilities for the leaders to include in their plans.

As long as there was still hope that the system could succeed, most Soviet people were willing to put up with its less attractive aspects, like the lack of personal freedom. But when it finally became obvious in the 1980s that the system was an economic failure, there was no good reason to keep it. The last Soviet leader, Mikhail Gorbachev, tried to make his country more democratic, but he was too late. By 1991, Stalin's system of central planning was being dismantled in all the countries in which it had been installed. It had failed to provide either a fairer or more efficient way of organizing society.

▲ A statue of Stalin lies broken on the ground after the fall of Communism in the Soviet Union in 1991.

Today

And yet, despite the failure, Stalin remains a popular figure for many people, particularly in Russia. Why is this? Why should a man who imposed so many sacrifices on others, and yet still failed to produce a successful system, still have his picture carried through the streets of Moscow?

The transition to democracy has been difficult, and life in present-day Russia is chaotic and uncertain. Ordinary people thought they knew where they were with Stalin. They knew they had a job, that the streets were safe, that as long as they kept their heads down there would be no knock on the door. There was order. They were being looked after. And during Stalin's day, the Soviet Union was becoming richer and more powerful daily. In the prison camps beyond the Arctic Circle, millions were being worked to death, but for most Russians the future may have seemed more promising then than it does today.

▶ *This photograph is from a Communist rally in Moscow in July 1999. More than 46 years after Stalin's death, these demonstrators still waved a red flag with his image on it.*

Timeline

1878	Soso Djugashvili (later called Stalin) is born in Gori. Until recently, it was thought that he was born in 1879.
1893	Djugashvili attends the theological seminary (school for training priests) in Tiflis.
1898	Russian Social Democratic Workers Party is formed.
1899	Djugashvili is expelled from the seminary and gets a job at the Tiflis observatory.
1901	After helping to organize a political demonstration in Tiflis, Djugashvili finds himself on the run from the police.
1902	After organizing a demonstration in Batum, Djugashvili is arrested and exiled to Siberia.
1903	Russian Social Democratic Workers Party splits into **Bolshevik** and **Menshevik** parties.
1904	Djugashvili returns to Tiflis and marries Ektarina.
1905	Djugashvili meets Lenin for the first time in Finland.
1906	His first son, Yakov, is born.
1907	Djugashvili organizes, and probably takes part in, the Erevan Square gold robbery. His first wife dies of illness.
1908–12	He is arrested, exiled, and manages to escape four times.
1913	Djugashvili meets Lenin in Kraków and travels to Vienna with him. With Lenin's help, he writes "Marxism and the National Question," signing it "Stalin"—his new name. Back in Russia he is arrested again.
1914	World War I begins.
1917	First Russian revolution takes place in February. Stalin travels to Moscow. Second Russian revolution—the Bolshevik revolution—takes place in October.
1918	Stalin marries Nadezhda Alliluyeva.

FOR DETAILS ON KEY PEOPLE OF STALIN'S TIME, SEE PAGES 58–59.

1918–21	Russian civil war takes place. Stalin is sent first to Tsaritsyn, and then to Petrograd and the Ukraine.
1921	Stalin's second son, Vasili, is born.
1922	Stalin becomes General Secretary of the **Communist** Party.
1924	Lenin dies in January, leaving a *Testament* critical of Stalin. Other party leaders choose to ignore it.
1925–27	In alliance with Bukharin, Stalin defeats the "Left Opposition" led by Trotsky and Zinoviev.
1926	Stalin's daughter, Svetlana, is born.
1927–29	Stalin defeats the so-called "Right Opposition" led by Bukharin.
1928–29	The first **five-year plan** is formulated.
1929–33	The **collectivization of agriculture** takes place. The "liquidation of the **kulaks**" takes place.
1932	Stalin's second wife, Nadezhda, commits suicide.
1934	Stalin uses Sergei Kirov's assassination in Leningrad as an excuse to begin a **purge** of the party.
1936	Stalin sends "volunteers" to fight in the **Spanish Civil War.**
1937–39	**Red Army** purges take place.
1938	The Munich Conference takes place.
1939	Stalin signs the **Nazi–Soviet Pact** with Hitler.
1941	Germany attacks the Soviet Union. German armies are stopped at the gates of Leningrad and Moscow.
1942	The second great German offensive is stopped at Stalingrad.
1943–45	The Red Army slowly forces the German army back to Berlin. Stalin meets the other two allied leaders at Tehran (1943), Yalta (1945), and Potsdam (1945).
1945	World War II ends. The U.S. ends the **Lend-Lease** program.
1947	The **Cold War** begins in earnest.
1948	Stalin purges the party in Leningrad.
1953	Stalin dies at the age of 75.

Key People of Stalin's Time

Beria, Lavrenti (1899–1953). Beria was a Georgian supporter of Stalin and head of the Soviet secret police from 1938. After Stalin's death, Beria was accused of attempting to seize power and was executed.

Bukharin, Nikolai Ivanovich (1888–1938). Born in Moscow, Bukharin became politically active as a student during the 1905 revolution. He lived as a **revolutionary** inside Russia until 1911, when he was arrested and **exiled.** He escaped to western Europe and returned to Russia in 1917. While there was a chance for further revolutions in Europe he argued for the **Bolsheviks** to make trouble wherever they could, but when it became clear that these revolutions would not take place, he joined first Lenin and then Stalin in arguing for a slow and peaceful progress toward **Socialism** in Russia. He was eventually driven from power when Stalin decided to adopt the faster method of modernizing the country. In 1938, he was the main figure in the last of the great **show trials,** and was shot soon afterward.

Churchill, Sir Winston (1874–1965). Churchill was a British politician. During the 1930s, he spoke out against the policies of successive leaders in his party. He became prime minister during the crucial early phase of World War II, and proved an inspirational figure in the British defiance of Nazi Germany.

Hitler, Adolf (1889–1945). Hitler was the leader of the German National Socialist, or Nazi, Party (1921–45) and Führer **(dictator)** of Germany from 1933 until he committed suicide in April 1945. Hitler restored the German economy and German pride through rearmament and an aggressive determination to retrieve territory lost in World War I. He was primarily responsible for the outbreak of World War II and the killing of 6 million Jews in German-occupied Europe.

Lenin, Vladimir Ilyich (1870–1924). Lenin was born Vladimir Ilyich Ulyanov. While practicing law in **St. Petersburg,** Lenin's interest in revolutionary politics developed. He was exiled to Siberia (1897–1900), and spent the following seventeen years living in western Europe. He was a deep thinker and wrote a great deal about politics and economics. He provoked the split in the Russian Social Democratic Workers Party in 1903 and became the undisputed leader of the Bolshevik Party. He returned to Russia in March 1917 and led the revolution in October that brought the Bolsheviks to power. Soon after the civil war had been won in 1921 he became ill, and he spent much of his last two years worrying about where the revolution was headed. He died in January 1924, leaving behind a *Testament* that suggested the removal of Stalin from his post as party general secretary.

Marx, Karl (1818–83). Marx was a German philosopher, economist, and political scientist whose theories of social development helped to inspire both Socialism and **Communism.**

Molotov, Vyacheslav (1890–1986). Molotov was an early member of the Bolsheviks, who became a firm supporter of Stalin after Lenin's death. He was Soviet foreign minister from 1939 to 1949 and from 1953 to 1956.

Trotsky, Leon (1879–1940). Trotsky was born Lev Davidovich Bronstein in Yanovka, Ukraine. As a young Jewish revolutionary, he was arrested and exiled to Siberia in 1898. He escaped to western Europe in 1902, but returned to play a starring role as leader of the St. Petersburg Soviet (Council) of Workers' Deputies in the 1905 Russian revolution. A great speaker and writer, he worked as a journalist in the West until 1917, when he returned again to Russia. He joined the Bolsheviks, supported Lenin when he argued for a Bolshevik revolution, and played a major role in bringing that revolution about. As Lenin's Commissar of War he created the **Red Army** and led it to victory in the civil war. After Lenin's death he argued for spreading the revolution to other countries, and was eased from power by jealous colleagues and the single-minded Stalin. Though expelled from the Soviet Union in 1929, he continued to oppose Stalin in his writings. In 1940, he was killed by one of Stalin's agents in Mexico.

Zinoviev, Grigory (1883–1936). Zinoviev was one of the most important Bolshevik leaders before the revolution. He was head of the Communist International, the association of national Communist Parties, from 1919 to 1926. He supported Stalin against Trotsky after Lenin's death, but was then defeated by an alliance of Stalin and Bukharin. He was executed by Stalin after the first of the great show trials in 1936.

Sources for Further Research

Downing, David. *Benito Mussolini.* Chicago: Heinemann Library, 2001.

Rappaport, Helen. *Joseph Stalin: A Biographical Companion.* Santa Barbara, Calif.: ABC-CLIO, Inc., 1999.

Reynoldson, Fiona. *Key Battles of World War II.* Chicago: Heinemann Library, 2001.

Reynoldson, Fiona. *Winston Churchill.* Chicago: Heinemann Library, 2001.

Ross, Stewart. *The U.S.S.R. under Stalin.* Danbury, Conn.: Franklin Watts Inc., 1991.

Serge, Victor. *Memoirs of a Revolutionary.* New York: Writers & Readers Publishing, Inc., 1984.

Siegelbaum, Lewis H. and Andrei Sokolov, eds. Translated by Thomas H. Hoisington and Steven Shabad. *Stalinism as a Way of Life: A Narrative in Documents.* New Haven, Conn.: Yale University Press, 2000.

Taylor, David. *Adolf Hitler.* Chicago: Heinemann Library, 2001.

Taylor, David. *The Cold War.* Chicago: Heinemann Library, 2001.

Taylor, David. *Franklin D. Roosevelt.* Chicago: Heinemann Library, 2001.

Willoughby, Susan. *The Russian Revolution.* Chicago: Heinemann Library, 1997.

Fiction

Orwell, George. *Animal Farm.* Hauppauge, N.Y.: Barron's Educational Series, Inc., 1999.

Glossary

anti-Fascist popular front alliance of Social Democrats and Communists against Fascists

autonomous having some degree of self-government inside a wider political body

black market unofficial, and often illegal, buying and selling

Bolsheviks one of the two political parties that emerged from the 1903 split in the Russian Social Democratic Workers Party. *Bolshevik* is Russian for "those with a majority."

bourgeoisie the capitalist class—those who own the industries and banks

Central Committee after 1917, the committee elected by local Communist Party committees throughout the Soviet Union

civil war war between different groups in one country

Cold War name given to the hostility that existed between the free enterprise and Communist worlds between 1945 and 1991

collectivization of agriculture the creation of large, jointly-owned farms by putting together small farms, which had previously been privately owned

Commissar for Nationalities position of authority with particular responsibility for relations among the different ethnic groups that made up the population of the Soviet Union

Communism according to Karl Marx, the stage of history that would follow Socialism. In this stage, free people would share with each other in a situation of economic plenty. The name was adopted by the Bolsheviks, and came to be associated with the system of economic planning and political dictatorship developed in the Soviet Union in the mid–twentieth century. A communist is a person who agrees with the ideas of Communism.

Cossacks a people of southern Russia

czar (or tsar) hereditary ruler of the Russian Empire before the revolution of 1917

dacha Russian country cottage used as a weekend or holiday home

delegate elected representative

dictatorship government by an individual (called a dictator) or small group that does not allow the mass of the people any say

European Russia that part of Russia lying to the west of the Ural Mountains (see map on page 13)

exile to be sent away as punishment. In czarist Russia, exile to remote and inhospitable parts of the country, like Siberia, was a common punishment.

Fascism dictatorial system of government that came to be known for its aggressive nationalism. A fascist is someone who agrees with the ideas of Fascism.

five-year plan plan for all intended economic activity over a five-year period. The first Soviet five-year plan was formulated in 1928 by Stalin.

free enterprise organization of economy where individuals, rather than governments, make the decisions about what goods and services are produced and how they are bought and sold

hypothermia subnormal temperature of the body

ideological difference disagreement over ideas, such as how economies and societies should be organized

industrial goods goods made from raw materials or other goods in factories or workshops

Kremlin walled fortress in Moscow that has been the traditional home of Russian leaders through the centuries

kulak rich peasant—in many cases, an employer of other peasants

labor camp camp where prisoners were forced to work

Lend-Lease program of American aid to those countries fighting the Germans in World War II, which began even before the U.S. entered the war in 1941

market rate price that a buyer and seller would agree on if there was no intervention from government

Marshall Plan huge program of American aid to the countries of Europe, proposed in 1947 and put into operation from 1948 to 1952

Marxist Socialist Socialist who believes and acts according to the theories of Karl Marx (see information boxes on pages 11 and 16)

Mensheviks one of the two political parties that emerged from the 1903 split in the Russian Social Democratic Workers Party. *Menshevik* is Russian for "those in a minority."

modernization bringing up to date by making use of the most advanced technology available

Munich Conference conference held in September 1938 to decide the future of Czechoslovakia, after Germany had threatened to invade that country. Britain and France offered a compromise, which gave the Germans only a part of the country.

Nazi–Soviet Pact treaty signed by Nazi Germany and the Soviet Union in August 1939.

They agreed not to attack each other and to remain neutral if the other was involved in a war with another country.

peasant farmer or worker on a small farm

personality cult campaign of exaggerated praise for an individual

planned economy economy in which all decisions are made by a central authority, and not by the free workings of the market

Politburo Soviet cabinet (or small ruling committee elected by the Central Committee)

political police police concerned with stopping real or imagined threats to the government

purge in a political party, a clearing out of unacceptable members. In Stalin's time this often involved having them killed.

Red Army originally the army formed by the Bolsheviks to defend their revolution in the civil war. After the civil war it became the official army of the Soviet Union.

Red Guards armed supporters of the Bolshevik revolution in its early years

reign of terror sustained campaign of violence and intimidation

revolutionary in politics, working to overthrow the existing order in its entirety—

not just swapping one group of individuals for another

St. Petersburg city on the Gulf of Finland and capital of the Russian Empire. Renamed Petrograd in 1914, Leningrad in 1924, and St. Petersburg once more in 1991.

show trial unfair trial held in public, simply to make a point to those outside the courtroom

smallpox serious and often fatal disease, common in the late nineteenth century

Socialism way of organizing society that puts the needs of the community above the short-term wants or needs of the individual. A socialist is someone who agrees with the ideas of Socialism.

Spanish Civil War civil war (1936–39) in Spain between republican government forces (mostly Socialists and Communists) and rebel Fascist forces

underground war when opponents of a government try to operate a hidden campaign, keeping their identity and whereabouts secret

White Army army fighting against the Bolsheviks in the civil war. Some members of the White Army wanted to bring back the czar; others to restore the government that existed between the two revolutions in 1917.

Index